Secrets of Blissful Life

ASHWIN SEBASTIAN

DEDICATION

This book is a heartfelt tribute to all those who seek a path to inner peace. May these pages be a guiding light, illuminating the way to a life filled with serenity, clarity, and profound joy. Your curiosity, open heart, and unwavering spirit have inspired me to explore the secrets that lead to happiness. Thank you for being a constant source of inspiration and for always reminding me of the beauty in every moment. May it inspire you to deepen your practice, expand your consciousness, and cultivate a profound sense of presence this dedication is a tribute to your courage and your commitment to finding solace within. May these pages offer you solace, guidance, and inspiration as you embark on your own journey towards uncovering the secrets of a blissful existence.

CONTENTS

ACKNOWLEDGMENTS

First and foremost, I would like to express my deepest gratitude to everyone who has contributed to the creation of this book. Without your support, encouragement, and expertise, this project would not have been possible. Special thank you to my mentors who have guided me on this transformative path and your wisdom and teachings have inspired me. I extend sincere appreciation to the editors, and everyone involved in the production of this book. Your meticulous attention to detail and commitment to excellence have transformed this project into a valuable resource for readers.

To all those who have played a role, big or small, in the creation of this book, please accept my deepest appreciation. To all those mentioned above and to anyone, whose contributions may have inadvertently been omitted, please accept my heartfelt appreciation. This book is the result of a collective effort, and I am truly grateful for your essential role in bringing it to fruition. Last but not least, I would like to acknowledge the readers of this book. It is your curiosity, enthusiasm, and eagerness to learn that have inspired me to delve into the depths of the topic and deliver a comprehensive exploration of the secrets of blissful life.

Thank you all.

Sincerely,

Ashwin Sebastian

1 BATH

Bathing is an important lifestyle which helps to clean the body as well as mind. According to Dharmashastra there are different type of bath based on time duration such as Munisnanam, Devasnanam, Manushyasnanam and Rakshasisnanam. The word Snanam means bath. According to Ayurveda, the hours before sunrise and before sunset are ideal for bathing. Bathing in different time duration will help to get different benefits such as good health, immunity, intellect, concentration, prosperity, mental peace, luck and happiness. If we bath between 4 am and 5 am known as Munisnanam. A bath during this time helps you to get good health, enjoy pleasure, intelligence, immunity from diseases and concentration. When you bath between 5 am and 6 am called as Devasnanam. If we bath during this time will helps to get prosperity, fame, mental peace and a comfortable life.

Next is Manushyasnanam the time is between 6 am and 8 am and bath based on this time duration 6 am and 8 am helps you to get luck, unity and happiness. Other bath is Rakshasisnanam Everybody should avoid bath after 8 in the morning. If you are unable to bath before 8 am, do so just before sunset. A bath after 8 am is termed Rakshasisnanam which lead to poverty, difficulties, loss of money according to ancient science. So, everybody should avoid bath after 8 am. I suggest Devasnanam, bath between 5 am and 6 am and Ayurveda prescribe two baths a day before sunrise and prior to sunset. You should take coconut oil in a transparent bottle and look into oil in the bottle and chant Om health overall health tranquility happiness compassion happiness awareness Aham awareness little bit loudly in three times daily before the bath and apply that oil little to the hair on head and all over to the body with your full awareness on hands movement and bath with full awareness or consciousness. If you too much cold outside bath in mild hot water.

According to Vastu Shastra, the wash basin and shower should be placed in the east moreover you should bath toward east direction is better. Before bath, chant Health overall Health tranquility happiness compassion happiness awareness Aham awareness three times into water in bathtub. Here not chant Om, Ya, Ru, Va And after this mantra, then get inside the bathtub and close your eyes then focus on lips for one minute. Do not think anything just focuses one minute on lips without mudras later do not think anything without any focus on anywhere for two minutes. Total three minutes meditation, one minute of focus on lips then two minutes without focus anywhere, relax in bathtub without any thoughts.

If you do not have bathtub, look to shower and chant this mantra health overall health tranquility happiness compassion happiness awareness Aham awareness three times then bath under shower facing toward east. If you do not have shower, look into water in bucket, chant health overall health tranquility happiness compassion happiness awareness Aham awareness three times into water in bucket then use that water for bath. Every day before you bath, chant this mantra, health overall health tranquility happiness compassion happiness awareness Aham awareness three times into water in bathtub or shower or water in bucket here not chant Om, Ya,Ru,Va and always bath facing toward east direction moreover bath twice a day is better. If any religious prayer before bath, you can chant religious prayer with this mantra otherwise you can ignore this mantra and bath with full awareness or consciousness facing toward east direction is better.

2 LUCKY BAMBOOS

Lucky Bamboo is the one of the most popular plant in Feng Shui which brings good luck and prosperity and other benefits based on the stalks. Each stalk provides different benefits. It is also known to enhance the flow of good energy in the home and office when placed in the right direction. It attracts money and wealth if kept in the southeast corner of the home entrance. And lucky bamboo is not a true bamboo Moreover, it can be grown in fresh water and that water must change weekly. Never use chlorine water for Lucky Bamboo and Lucky Bamboo helps to keep the environment clean because it purify air and provide more oxygen to the surrounding environment by absorb carbon dioxide and release oxygen. Take a small flower pot fill with water and put stalks in to flower pot. Keep the flower pot with Lucky Bamboo over the wooden stand in the southeast corner of the home entrance is believed to bring wealth and prosperity in the home.

It can grow both bright light as well as lower light. Always check the water level in pot and do not let the lucky bamboo dry out furthermore keep the root covered with water at all times. Only healthy and green lucky bamboo brings prosperity so remove if any part of the leaves yellow or dry which helps to stop to spread to the entire plant.

Lucky bamboo stalks and its benefits.

1 stalks: meaningful life

2 stalks: luck in love and marriage

3 stalks: happiness

4 stalks: avoid four stalks because four could draw negative energy according to Chinese   culture

5 stalks: creativity and academic achievement

6 stalks: blessing

7 stalks: health

8 stalks: bring wealth

9 stalks: good fortune and overall luck

10 stalks: perfection or completeness

21 stalks: blessing and abundance

88 stalks: doubling of joy

289 stalks: luck or good fortune come easily

If you wish to buy lucky bamboo you should take plastic red color small flower pot, fill with water and take 8 stalks or more and put some rocks or pebbles inside the flower pot furthermore tie lucky bamboo with red ribbon not too much tight and it keep over the wooden stand in the southeast corner of the home entrance

3 AQUARIUMS

Everybody knows fish bowl and aquarium or fish tank. It is a transparent glass container filled with water in which people keep fish and other water creatures. Aquariums have both merit and demerit. According to vastu aquarium should be kept in north east corner or north east direction in your living room. I have aquarium past 5 years ago and I get some health issue because I keep it in the wrong position then I remove aquarium or fish tank from my home. Instead of aquarium lucky bamboo is better and you can buy lucky bamboo from aquarium shop.

4 SIDDHASANA

The term Siddha widely used in Indian culture. It means a perfected master or a yogi who achieved a high degree of physical as well as spiritual perfection or enlightenment. The term Asana means posture so practicing Siddhasana on a regular basis may help to reduce stress and symptoms associated with anxiety.

<u>Step to do Siddhasana</u>

- Sit straight with spine and neck erect in a yoga mat facing toward east.

- Bend the right leg and place the heel near the perineum and not touch perineum.

- Bend the left leg and place the left ankle over the right leg. Now place the left heel above the genitals and not touch genitals just near the genitals.

- Place the right toes in between the left calf muscle and thigh and left toes in between the right calf muscle and thigh.

- Place the hands on the knees in Prana mudra. If you feel discomfort for this Siddhasana you can practice other variation of Siddhasana.

Variation of Siddhasana

- Sit straight with spine and neck erect in Sukhasana or cross-legged easy pose in a yoga mat facing toward east.

- Bend the left leg over the right leg.

- Place the hands on the knees in Prana mudra.

If you have any health problems or any issue with your ankles or leg and if you feel any pain stop doing Siddhasana and also pregnant women should avoid this Siddhasana and variation of Siddhasana. Otherwise do Siddhasana for one minute in a day. I usually prefer variation of that siddhasana. When you do Siddhasana or variation of Siddhasana then close eyes and chant Om Health Overall Health Tranquility Happiness Compassion Happiness Awareness for a one minute with Prana mudra. If you are unable to do Siddhasana and variation of Siddhasana then sit straight in a comfortable chair, place the hands on the knees in Prana mudra and chant Om Health Overall Health Tranquility Happiness Compassion Happiness Awareness for a one minute.

5 CUMIN SEEDS WATER

Cumin seed have many health benefits and there are many types of cumin such are black cumin, fennel is also other type of cumin and people mainly use this seeds for cooking food. it also have medicinal properties, take half small spoon of cumin seed not fennel or black cumin and add into 8 glass of water and boil cumin and water together for a 15 minutes after the temperature of water lower and drink that water gradually in everyday with mantra, do not use cumin seed water after 8 hours because boiled cumin seed water become decay after 8 hours so drink gradually within 8 hours.

<u>Health benefits of cumin</u>

- cumin contain antioxidants
- help to control blood sugar
- antibacterial properties
- anti-inflammatory properties
- boost memory
- Promotes digestion
- promotes weight loss
- good for skin
- may help lower cholesterol

When you wake up in morning, take 2 glass cumin seeds water and look into cumin seeds water and chant one time Om health overall health tranquility happiness Ya compassion happiness Ru compassion wealth happiness happiness happiness Va health awareness Ha awareness in low voice or in your mind. When you chant this mantra visualize last word awareness on lips into cumin seeds water and when you drink that water concentrate the way of movement of water from mouth to stomach. This process helps to improve your awareness or consciousness and always aware your movements of hands and body in that whole day. Chant this mantra only after age of 15 years.

Chant that mantra daily into water, coffee, tea and all drinks but do not chant that mantra into alcohol and beer. In alcohol and beer avoid sound Om, Ya, Ru and Va. So chant one time in alcohol and beer like health overall health tranquility happiness compassion happiness awareness Ha awareness. If you have religious prayer into drink, you can also chant this mantra into drink otherwise just ignore this mantra and only chant religious prayer. When you drink concentrate the way of movement of cumin seeds water from mouth to stomach that also helps to improve awareness or consciousness Moreover, religious prayer always better. When you chant this mantra then drink yourself fully immediately. Do not share that water or other drinks to anybody or any living organism. If you want to share water or drink to others, share without chant this mantra into drinks or water then share to others or other living organism.

6 MANTRA INTO FOODS

When you have food avoid facing toward south, south is not good direction for eat food. According to vastu shastra when you eat facing toward the east direction promote better digestion and health furthermore west direction good for business people and professionals.When you have food facing toward north direction helpful for knowledge and money. I suggest have food facing toward east direction. Before have food look into food chant one time OM health overall health tranquility happiness YA compassion happiness RU compassion wealth happiness happiness happiness VA health awareness AHAM awareness in low voice or in your mind. When you chant this mantra visualise last word of awareness on lips into food and concentrate chewing of food and when you swallow food just concentrate the way of movement of food from mouth to stomach continuously every time when you eat food. It helps to increase your awareness or consciousness.

If you have religious prayer into food, you can chant prayers with this mantra otherwise ignore this mantra. Only chant religious prayer and concentrate chewing of food and when you swallow food, just concentrate way of movement of food from mouth to stomach and Concentrate continuously every time when you eat food. Which help to increase your awareness or consciousness Moreover, religious prayer are always better when you have non-vegetarian food just avoid sound OM, YA and VA.

So just chant one time health overall health tranquility happiness compassion happiness Ru compassion wealth happiness happiness happiness health awareness AHAM awareness into non-vegetarian food. When you chant this mantra into food, then you should eat that food fully so never share that food with mantra to anybody or any living organism. If you want to share to others or other living organism, then share the food without mantra.

.

7 BREATH OF FIRE PRANAYAMA

Breath of fire is a breathing exercise and inhale hold one second then exhale little bit forcefully through nose, here only 3 counts is enough and pregnant ladies and people with heart disease should avoid breath of fire pranayama.

<u>Steps to do breath of fire pranayama</u>

- sit straight with spine and neck erect in sukhasana or cross legged easy pose in a yoga mat facing toward east
- place your hands palms facing upwards on knees and close your eyes
- inhale through your nose and hold one second
- exhale through nose little forcefully by belly
- Repeat 3 time, here 3 time is enough

<u>Health benefits of breath of fire pranayama</u>

- stress reduction
- better concentration
- good for digestion etc

You can also learn breath of fire pranayama in @justovercome YouTube channel.

8 RING

Our fingers in hands represents different planets if you get any bad energy from any planets then wear ring on different fingers helpful to protect us from bad energy from planets. index finger represent planet Jupiter, middle finger represent planet Saturn and ring finger represent Sun. according to astrology if Saturn is wrong position in your horoscope then wear iron ring or stainless steel ring on middle finger that remove negative energy from planet Saturn. When you wear iron ring or steel ring on middle finger then you must wear iron ring or steel ring on index finger.

The metal of planet Saturn is iron if you do not get iron ring then wear steel. the metal of planet Jupiter is gold according to Veda those who wear gold never fall in ill so wear gold ring on index finger with steel ring so wear two ring on index finger first one is gold ring then wear steel ring.

If you need to get protection from planet Saturn then men should wear one iron or stainless steel ring on middle finger and one gold ring and one stainless steel ring on index finger of right hand moreover wear gold ring on left hand ring finger. Female should wear one iron or stainless steel ring on left hand middle finger and wear one gold ring and one stainless steel ring on index finger of left hand and wear gold ring on right hand ring finger.

In our body right side denote Surya nadi which represent men and left side denote Chandra nadi which represent female. So wear men and women ring on above manner moreover you can also wear gold ring on ring fingers of both hands. you can chant mantra by look into ring every day morning and chant without OM, YA, RU, VA, HA and AHAM like health overall health tranquility happiness compassion happiness awareness to all rings one time little loudly and wear it. When you have food remove all ring after food wear all ring on hands furthermore when you sleep remove ring on index finger and middle finger and in morning chant mantra into all ring and wear it.

9 PRANAYAMA ONE

Pranayama is a breathing exercise for physical and mental wellness. The term prana means life energy and yama means control. Pranayama have many health benefits moreover it reduce stress and improve sleep quality. It involves inhalation, exhalation and hold breath. Here explaining a type of pranayama and adding some word Om health health health health health health while doing pranayama.

<u>Steps to do pranayama</u>

- Sit straight with spine and neck erect in sukhasana or cross-legged easy pose in a yoga mat facing toward east

- Close your eyes

- Place your left hand in chin mudra over thigh

- Place your right hand in nasika mudra

- Inhale first through left nostril

- Close the right nostril by using thumb of nasika mudra then inhale deeply and slowly through left nostril. When inhale chant in your mind Om health health health health health health. Total chant six time health after Om. Then exhale through right nostril. When exhale do not chant anything.

- Again, inhale through left nostril and chant in mind OM health health health health health health Total chant health 6 times after OM. Then exhale through right nostril. While exhale do not chant anything.

- Again, inhale through left nostril and chant in mind, OM health health health health health health. Then exhale through right nostril.

- Close the left nostril using Nasik Mudra, Ring Finger and Pinkie and inhale through right nostril. When inhale, chant OM health health health health health health in mind. Total chant 6 time health after OM. Then exhale through left nostril. Do not chant anything while exhale.

- Again, inhale through right nostril and chant in mind, OM health health health health health health. Total chant health 6 times after OM. Then exhale through left nostril.

- Again inhale through right nostril, chant in mind Om health health health health health health then exhale through left nostril.

- Here one round is completed. Three time inhale through left nostril and exhale through right nostril and three time inhale through right nostril and exhale through left nostril. Next is same process here hold breath for six second with mantra.

- close right nostril by using nasika mudra thumb then inhale through left nostril while inhale chant Om health health health health health health in mind. total chant health six time after Om and hold breath for six second then exhale through right nostril while exhale do not chant anything and do this two more time.

- after that close left nostril by using nasika mudra ring finger and pinkie and inhale through right nostril while inhale chant Om health health health health health health in mind and hold breath for six second then exhale through left nostril while exhale do not chant anything. Do this two more time here second round is completed.

People with heart problems and pregnant woman avoid this pranayama you can learn this pranayama in @justovercome YouTube channel.

10 MANTRA INTO PALM

Some people can tell your future by looks your line on palm because they believe brain vibration reflect line on a palm and this shastra known as hastrekha shastra or palmistry. Chant happiness health awareness into the center of palm of both hands one time little loudly without sound OM, YA, RU, VA, HA and AHAM. Chant happiness health awareness in this exact order. First chant happiness then health and last awareness into the center of palm one time in morning and night before sleep. After chant this into palm then always stays in presence of mind.

11 RASNADI CHURNAM

According to Ayurveda imbalance of tridosha lead to get disease.Tridosha are Vata, Kapha and Pitta. Rasnadi churnam balance Vata and Kapha dosha. Rasnadi churnam is an ayurvedic product moreover it have many health benefits and it is an ayurvedic powder for external use. After bath dry your hair with the help of towel and apply rasnadi churnam on top center of head or crown chakra with mantra. I am using kottakkal arya vaidya sala rasnadi churnam. Apply rasnadi churnam daily after the bath.

After bath first chant into both palms of hands happiness health awareness one time then take little rasnadi churnam into left hand then move left hand close to lips and chant OM health overall health tranquility happiness compassion happiness awareness AHAM awareness one time into rasnadi churnam without looking on it. Then take rasnadi churnam with the help of index finger and thumb of right hand and move right hand close to lips and again chant OM health overall health tranquility happiness compassion happiness awareness AHAM awareness one time and apply it into crown chakra or sahasrara chakra. Do this process daily after the bath. When you chant mantra into rasnadi churnam then not need to look into rasnadi churnam, just chant mantra without looking on it. When you apply rasnadi churnam into crown chakra then chant OM health overall health tranquility happiness compassion happiness awareness AHAM awareness one time in mind. After apply it then wash your hands to remove remaining rasnadi churnam from hands.

12 BHRAMARI PRANAYAMA

Bhramari Pranayama is a yogic breathing technique that involves producing a humming sound or N sound during exhalation. The name Bhramari comes from the Sanskrit word for black bee. Bhramari Pranayama has many potential benefits including reducing stress, anxiety, promote better sleep and it help to calm the mind.

<u>Steps to do Bhramari Pranayama</u>

- Sit in a comfortable cross-legged position with your spine straight and your eyes closed.

- Do Shanmukhi Mudra or place your thumbs over your ears and your index fingers over your eyebrows then other three fingers over your closed eyes that not need to touch eyes.

- Inhale slowly and deeply as you exhale make gentle humming sound or N sound.

- Repeat 21 times.

- After 21 time chant happiness for 3 times then open your eyes.

Pregnant women, people with heart disease and ear pain should be avoid this Bhramari Pranayama. You can learn Bhramari Pranayama in @justovercome YouTube channel.

13 SLEEP

A good sleep is required for the physical health and mental health. Everybody knows a person should need 7 to 9 hours sleep Furthermore people should have food at least 3 hours before sleep. Chant some mantra before sleep so sit straight with spine and neck erect in sukhasana or cross-legged easy pose in yoga mat facing toward east and place hands on knees in prana mudra then chant OM health overall health tranquility happiness compassion happiness awareness for one minute without YA, RU, VA, HA and AHAM

After that lay on bed and close your eyes then inhale deeply when you inhale chant in mind wealth wealth wealth then hold breath seven seconds then exhale.Again inhale deeply while inhale chant in mind wealth three time and hold breath seven seconds then exhale and again inhale deeply while inhale chant in mind wealth wealth wealth and hold seven seconds then exhale.Total three inhalation and exhalation after inhalation and exhalation then chant I am healthy person, I am wealthy person and I am happy person for three time.Do this daily before sleep.After chant this mantra then sleep well.

According to Vastu Shastra when you sleep in bed your head is pointed south and your feet are pointed north. Avoid head pointed to north for sleep. I refer sleep in bed your head is pointed south and your feet are pointed to north for better health.

14 THOUGHTS

Thoughts is an important tool if you face any problem now so just think how to overcome my all problems and how to get a blissful life 10 time repeatedly in a daily. After 10 times analyse any solution get. If get use that solution and continue to keep think like that morning and night before sleep. If you do not get any solution do not worry think that 10 time morning and night before sleep. It will naturally attract to overcome problems and get blissful life. When you think like that you may get many solutions to overcome your problems so all the solutions use in daily life later change thinking just think how to get blissful life and keep think morning and night 10 time and use solutions in life.

If you do not have any problems then just think how to get blissful life 10 time in morning and night before sleep and find out solutions to get blissful life and keep think how to get blissful life and use solutions in daily life to get blissful life.If do not get any solution do not worry keep think that morning and night 10 time.

15 NASIKA MUDRA

Nasika mudra is used in different pranayama and it is also called as Vishnu mudra. It is helpful to reduce anxiety. When we do pranayama left hand become in Chin mudra and right hand in Nasika mudra.

<u>Steps to do Nasika mudra</u>

- Sit straight with spine and neck erect in a yoga mat facing toward east.

- Place your left hand in chin mudra on thigh.

- Fold the index and middle fingers of right hand and touch the palm of right hand.

16 NADI SHUDDHI PRANAYAMA

Nadi Shuddhi Pranayama is a type of pranayama that purify energy channel in our body and astral body.It very helpful to reduce stress with many other health benefits. Nadi Shuddhi Pranayama is a breathing exercise without mantra but you can chant some mantra in mind while doing Nadi Shuddhi Pranayama for more benefits.

<u>Steps to do Nadi Shuddhi Pranayama with Mantra</u>

- Sit straight with spine and neck erect in sukhasana or cross-legged easy pose in a yoga mat facing toward east.

- Both hands thumb fingers tip touch to the end of ring fingers then Fold three fingers except index fingers and close your eyes.

- In this pranayama inhale first through left nostril.

- So close the right nostril with that right hand Index finger then inhale slowly and deeply through left nostril. When breath in chant in your mind awareness awareness awareness awareness awareness awareness. Here not chant OM in front of awareness and total 6 times chant awareness while inhale and exhale slowly through right nostril. When exhale do not chant anything.

- After that close the left nostril with left hand index finger and inhale slowly and deeply through right nostril. When breath in chant in your mind Awareness Awareness Awareness Awareness Awareness Awareness. Here not chant OM in front of awareness and total 6 times chant Awareness while inhale and exhale through left nostril slowly. When exhale do not chant anything.

- Repeat this for 30 minutes.

- Later inhale through both nostril then chant in mind awareness 3 times and hold 6 seconds then exhale through nose. Do this 3 times.

Gradually increase the time of this pranayama. First do this pranayama for 5 minutes then increase time of pranayama for 10 minutes and increase time till 30 minutes.

Do this pranayama with full awareness or consciousness and this pranayama is very important so everybody should definitely do this pranayama for 30 minutes. Pregnant women and people with heart disease should avoid this pranayama and you can also learn this pranayama and its mudra in @justovercome YouTube channel.

17 CHIN MUDRA

Chin mudra is an important mudra and the meaning of Chin in Sanskrit is Chitta which means consciousness. Chin mudra helps to reduce stress and anxiety. It is very useful to overcome bad thoughts and depression.

Steps to do Chin Mudra

- Sit straight with spine and neck erect in sukhasana or cross-legged easy pose in a yoga mat facing toward east.

- If you have uncomfortable to sit in sukhasana then sit in chair.

- Join the tip of index finger and thumb of both hands. Keep the other three fingers extended.

- Place chin mudra on thigh.

18 PRANA MUDRA

The term prana means life force energy and mudra is a gesture of hands and fingers.Prana mudra is very beneficial mudra which have many health benefits. It helps to overcome bad thoughts, improve immunity power, improve eyesight and helps to reduce diabetes.

Steps to do prana mudra

- Sit straight with spine and neck erect in sukhasana or cross-legged easy pose in a yoga mat facing toward east.

- If you have uncomfortable to sit in sukhasana then sit in chair.

- Allow hands to rest on the thighs and join tip of the little finger, ring finger and thumb. Keep other two fingers extended.

19 SWEAT AND ZAFU

Sweat

When we do any exercise then our sweat gland produce sweat and the studies says sweat contain dermcidin peptide which helps to fight infection because dermcidin peptide can kill bacteria and virus. Everybody know if we do exercise the chance to get infection are comparatively less so if your health is good to do exercise then do any exercise to prevent infection. After sweat wait 30 minutes to dry off sweat and cool down then do shower.

Zafu

Zafu or small meditation cushion can use during pranayama which helps to do pranayama or meditation for long period of time. So take a yoga mat and keep zafu on it and sit over the zafu then do pranayama or meditation. Zafu helps to sitting positions more stable.

20 PLANT TREE

Plant different trees in some directions will bring prosperity. There is an old story that tells if we plant gooseberry tree in north side of land or house when gooseberry tree grow, then the wealth of owner become increase. When you plant tree then keep at least 10 meter away from the house for safety of house. Everybody know all trees are not grow everywhere because of climate. But this is just a traditional knowledge so plant bamboo in south eastern corner and plant jack trees in east. Moreover plant gooseberry tree and mango tree in north side. Furthermore plant tamarind in south side and in west side plant turmeric.Plant golden shower tree in north east corner for prosperity. If you wish to plant trees then avoid chant mantras in that day then plant trees.

21 LAUGHING MEDITATION

Laughing meditation is a simple breathing exercise and it includes breathing, hold breath and chant some words while inhale and everybody should do laughing meditation twice a day.

Steps to do Laughing Meditation

- Sit straight with spine and neck erect in sukhasana or cross-legged easy pose in a yoga mat facing toward east.

- If you have uncomfortable to sit in sukhasana then sit in chair.

- Allow hands to rest on the thighs with prana mudra and close your eyes.

- Inhale slowly and deeply while inhale chant in mind the word happiness for 7 times and hold 3 second then exhale through nose and do smile while exhale.

- Repeat this 7 times.

- After 7 times inhale again while inhale chant in mind happiness for 7 times then hold 3 second and while exhale laugh with little sound.

- Repeat this 7 times.

- Total 14 inhalation and exhalation.

Do laughing meditation daily in morning and night with lucky bamboo but pregnant women and people with heart disease avoid laughing meditation. You can learn this laughing meditation in @justovercome YouTube channel.

22 CLOVE WATER

Clove have antibacterial properties so before start breathing exercise, take 3 glass water and it boil with 1 teaspoon clove together for 15 minute after temperature of clove water very low then take that water into transparent spray bottle and chant OM health tranquility awareness awareness awareness AHAM awareness into clove water in a spray bottle.

Before breathing exercise or pranayama spray that water into the place you do breathing exercise or pranayama so spray that water into yoga mat or place near to yoga mat then do pranayama. After pranayama or breathing exercise again spray clove water the area you do pranayama. When chant mantra you do not look into spray bottle just move the spray bottle near to lips and chant OM health tranquility awareness awareness awareness AHAM awareness for three time.

23 SALT

Add pinch sea salt into the bathing water helps to get health. it good for skin, good for people who have arthritis, remove negative energy and many other benefits so bath in salt water once a week. Do not store salt in bathroom and take salt and chant happiness health awareness in low voice to salt three times and add salt into water for bath. Avoid pour salt water on head and face after salt water bath then pour normal water on head,face and body.

24 DRINK WATER FROM A PURE COPPER BOTTLE

Drinking water from a copper bottle offers a range of benefits for our health and well-being. Firstly, copper has antimicrobial properties that can help kill harmful bacteria and viruses. Additionally copper is known to have anti-inflammatory and antioxidant properties. Regular intake of water stored in a copper bottle can help to reducing inflammation in the body and help fight against cell-damaging free radicals moreover Drinking water from a copper bottle is believed to have a calming effect on the body and mind. Copper is known to have certain properties that can help reduce stress and anxiety.

Store water 8 hours in pure copper bottle or vessel then drink from it for more benefits and that water balance tridoshas such as vata, pitta and kapha. Ayurveda says imbalance of tridoshas lead to get disease.Furthermore, clean copper bottle or vessel weekly and drink water from copper bottle or vessel with mantra to water.

25 SINGING BOWLS

Singing bowl is a type of musical instrument and it is made of crystal or metal typically bronze or brass and has a flat bottom with a round body. The bowl is played by striking its rim or rubbing a wooden or felt-covered mallet along the rim. Singing bowls are believed to have healing and therapeutic properties, as the sound and vibrations they produce are said to promote balance and harmony within the body and mind. They are often used in sound therapy or meditation practices to induce a state of deep relaxation and to achieve a sense of inner peace.

Everyday time between 4 pm to 7: 30 pm, play 5 minute C note singing bowl after that play E note singing bowl. chant happiness health awareness into both hands palm and close your eyes then play singing bowl.C note singing bowl represent for muladhara chakra and E note singing bowl represent for manipura chakra moreover do not use others singing bowls and do not give your singing bowls to others.

26   ABHAYA VARADA MUDRA

The Abhaya Varada Mudra is believed to have several benefits. It is said to promote confidence and a sense of protection. This mudra is also help to calm the mind and reduce anxiety so Everyday time between 4 pm to 7: 30 pm, play 5 minute C note singing bowl after that play E note singing bowl after do abhaya varada mudra for 2 minute.

<u>Steps to practice Abhaya Varada Mudra</u>

- Sit in a comfortable seated position with your back straight and close your eyes.

- Raise your right hand to the level of the shoulder, keeping your elbow relaxed and your forearm parallel to the ground.

- Turn your right hand palm to face outward and your wrist should be straight.

- Keep your fingers of right hand pointing upwards.

- Place your left hand palm on left leg knee to face upwards.

27 MANTRAS

All this mantras only chant after 15 years old, smokers and pregnant women avoid chant this mantras furthermore after 8pm avoid chant sound OM, YA, RU, VA, HA and AHAM into the foods and drinks. You can chant mantras without OM, YA, RU, VA, HA and AHAM into foods and drinks after 8pm. Avoid chant this mantras half hours before and after sex moreover before sex and after sex sit in sukhasana with spine and neck straight then inhale through nose and hold breath as long as you can then exhale when you inhale breath chant in mind wealth love compassion and while exhale do not chant anything. Do this breathing exercise 7 time here inhalation and exhalation time should be same. Everybody definitely do this breathing exercise before and after sex furthermore couple can do this breathing exercise together if they wish.

- Mantra to oil: OM Health Overall Health Tranquility Happiness Compassion Happiness Awareness AHAM Awareness.

- Mantra into water in bathtub: Health Overall Health Tranquility Happiness Compassion Happiness Awareness AHAM Awareness 3 time, here not chant sound OM, YA, RU and VA

- Mantra to Shower: Health Overall Health Tranquility Happiness Compassion Happiness Awareness AHAM Awareness Three Time, Here Not Chant Sound OM, YA RU and VA.

- Mantra into Water in Bucket: Health Overall Health Tranquility Happiness Compassion Happiness Awareness AHAM Awareness Three Time Here also not Chant Sound OM, YA, RU and VA.

- Mantra in Siddhasana: OM Health Overall Health Tranquility Happiness Compassion Happiness Awareness. Chant it for one minute with Prana mudra.

- Mantra in Chair: OM Health Overall Health Tranquility Happiness Compassion Happiness Awareness. Chant it for one minute with Prana mudra.

- Mantra into Cumin Seeds Water or Mantra into Other Drinks except Alcohol and Beer: OM Health Overall Health Tranquility Happiness YA Compassion Happiness RU compassion wealth happiness happiness happiness VA Health Awareness HA Awareness. Visualise Last Word Awareness on Lips into Drinks.

- Mantra to Alcohol and Beer: Health Overall Health Tranquility Happiness Compassion happiness Awareness HA Awareness. Here do not chant OM, YA, RU and VA into Alcohol and Beer.

- Mantra to Vegetarian Food: OM Health Overall Health Tranquility Happiness YA Compassion Happiness RU Compassion wealth happiness happiness happiness VA Health Awareness AHAM Awareness. Visualise Last Word Awareness on Lips into Food.

- Mantra to Non-Vegetarian Food: Health Overall Health Tranquility Happiness Compassion Happiness RU compassion wealth happiness happiness happiness health Awareness AHAM Awareness. Here do not chant sound OM, YA and VA but Visualise Last Word Awareness on Lips into Food.

- Mantra to ring: health overall health tranquility happiness compassion happiness awareness. Here not chat, OM, YA, RU,VA, HA and AHAM

- Mantra in pranayama one: OM health health health health health health.

- Mantra into palm: Happiness health awareness.

- Mantra into rasnadi churnam: OM health overall health tranquility happiness compassion happiness awareness AHAM awareness.

- Mantra before sleep: OM health overall health tranquility happiness compassion happiness awareness here not chant sound YA,RU,VA,HA and AHAM.

- Mantra on bed: wealth wealth wealth after inhalation and exhalation I am healthy person, I am wealthy person and I am happy person.

- Mantra in nadi shuddhi pranayama: awareness awareness awareness awareness awareness awareness total chant awareness 6 time. Here not chant OM, YA, RU, VA, HA and AHAM.

- Mantra in Laughing Meditation: Happiness Happiness Happiness Happiness Happiness Happiness Happiness. Total Chant Happiness Seven time, here not chant OM,YA, RU,VA, HA and AHAM.

- Mantra into Clove Water: OM Health Tranquility Awareness Awareness Awareness AHAM Awareness.

- Mantra into Salt: Happiness Health Awareness

- Mantra into Food and Drinks after 8pm: Health Overall Health Tranquility Happiness Compassion Happiness Compassion Health Awareness Awareness.

28 LIFESTYLE OF BLISSFUL LIFE

Wake up between 5 a.m. and 6 a.m. and pour water on leg furthermore wash your hands, mouth and face then brush your teeth and do your morning routine then sit straight with spine and neck erect in sukhasana or cross-legged easy pose in a yoga mat or chair facing toward east and chant OM health overall health tranquility happiness compassion happiness awareness six time with prana mudra and take two glass of cumin seed water and chant into cumin seed water OM health overall health tranquility happiness YA compassion happiness RU compassion wealth happiness happiness happiness VA health awareness HA awareness and drink that water while drinking concentrate the way of movement of water from mouth to stomach.

After drinking cumin seed water, then apply oil with mantra and chant mantra into the water in bathtub. Then get inside the bathtub and close your eyes. Then focus on lips for one minute without mudra and do not think anything. Just focus one minute on lips, later two minute without any focus on anywhere and do not think anything for two minute. Total three minute meditation. One minute focus on lips then two minute without focus anywhere, relax in bathtub without any thoughts. After three minute bath yourself then apply rasnadi churnam in crown chakra with mantra.

Later spray the clove water with mantra into the place you do pranayama then sit straight with spine and neck erect in sukhasana or cross-legged easy pose over the zafu in a yoga mat facing toward east and take lucky bamboo then place it 1 meter in front of yoga mat which help to get more oxygen while do pranayama, always do pranayama in the environment have more oxygen and do breath of fire pranayama, here only need 3 inhalation and 3 exhalation.

After that do pranayama one with mantra. After finish pranayama one relax your legs for 3 minute. Later make sound saaa for 7 time. The sound saaa you can also find out in carnatic music and do nadi shuddhi pranayama with mantra for 30 minute. After finish nadi shuddhi pranayama then remove zafu from yoga mat and lay on yoga mat for 6 minute to relax legs. Then do bhramari pranayama with zafu. Later do laughing meditation with mantra. Then lay on yoga mat for 6 minute and sit in variation of siddhasana and chant OM health overall health tranquility happiness compassion happiness awareness for 1 minute with prana mudra.

Then move Lucky Bamboo into South eastern corner of home entrance. Later spray the clove water with mantra again into the place you do pranayama and breathing exercise. Finally, chant Happiness Health Awareness one time into the center of palm of both hands. Moreover, drink black coffee with mantra after pranayama and breathing exercise.

Do this process daily and you can also adopt other methods to overcome negative thought. If you eat food then only do pranayama and breathing exercise after 3 hours. In your free time think how to get blissful life 10 time and also in morning and night before sleep. Do laughing meditation with lucky bamboo half hour before sleep in night. Laughing meditation is important so everybody should do laughing meditation daily in morning and night with lucky bamboo.

ABOUT THE AUTHOR

Ashwin Sebastian is an accomplished writer and has been passionately engaged in the world of literature for over two years. With a unique perspective and a knack for writing, Ashwin Sebastian has crafted an impressive body of work that has captivated readers from all walks of life. Born in kerala, Ashwin Sebastian discovered their love for writing at an early age, inspired by the world around them. They honed their skills through extensive study, earning a degree in logistics from Bharathiar University.

Ashwin Sebastian aims to transport readers to captivating worlds, inspire introspection, and provoke meaningful conversations. Their commitment to providing readers with an unforgettable reading experience is evident in every meticulously written word.